12/18

# THE
# country
# HOME

*Simona Hill*

# THE
# country
# HOME

*Decorative details and delicious recipes*

LORENZ BOOKS

This edition is published by Lorenz Books

Lorenz Books is an imprint of
Anness Publishing Ltd
Hermes House
88–89 Blackfriars Road
London SE1 8HA
tel. 020 7401 2077; fax 020 7633 9499
www.lorenzbooks.com; info@anness.com

This edition distributed in the UK by
The Manning Partnership Ltd
6 The Old Dairy, Melcombe Road
Bath BA2 3LR
tel. 01225 478 444; fax 01225 478 440

This edition distributed in the USA and
Canada by
National Book Network
4501 Forbes Boulevard
Suite 200, Lanham, MD 20706
tel. 301 459 3366; fax 301 429 5746
www.nbnbooks.com

This edition distributed in Australia by
Pan Macmillan Australia
Level 18, St Martins Tower
31 Market St
Sydney, NSW 2000
tel. 1300 135 113; fax 1300 135 103
customer.service@macmillan.com.au

PUBLISHER: Joanna Lorenz
MANAGING EDITOR: Helen Sudell
PROJECT EDITOR: Simona Hill
DESIGNER: Louise Clements
EDITORIAL READER: Lindsay Zamponi
PRODUCTION CONTROLLER: Darren Price

10 9 8 7 6 5 4 3 2 1

# Contents

Introduction     6

*Country Style*     8
    Plain & Simple Hues     12
    Neutral Tones     14
    Prints & Weaves     16
    Simple Motifs     18
    Country Finishes     20

*Country Crafts*     22
    Tactile Textiles     26
    Easy Embroidery     28
    Tincraft & Wirework     30
    Pressed Flowers     32
    Country Prints     34

*Country Gifts*     36
    Twigs & Pebbles     40
    Welcoming Garlands     42
    Pretty Posies     44
    Seasonal Icons     46
    Decorative Drying     48

*The Kitchen*     50
    Afternoon Tea     54
    Breads & Teabreads     56
    Old-fashioned Desserts     58
    Biscuits & Cookies     60
    Sweets & Candies     62

Index     64

# Introduction

The appeal of a country-style home is based on much more than the veneer of interior design. It is the lifestyle that people try to recreate in their homes; the kind of cosy, pastoral idyll that they associate with rural life in bygone years: a far cry, no doubt, from the realities of what was essentially a working lifestyle. In the country-style home, the boundaries between indoors and outdoors are blurred. In the summer, we take our living space into the garden, and during all seasons, we can bring a little of the outside in. Nature is often reflected in the furnishings we choose and the decorations we make. Homes would once have been furnished with wooden furniture made from timber that would have been sourced, carved and manufactured locally. Walls would have been painted with soft, muted colours, manufactured from natural pigments; and soft furnishings would have been stitched at home, using any fabric to hand. The design would depend on the maker's skill and ingenuity. Country style has developed from this interdependence on the land. However, country-style homes need not be confined to rural locations. Even in the city, the most urban home can be decorated and furnished with the essence of country charm.

*Enhance your tea tray with decorated linens, such as this pretty napkin with its daisy motif.*

Country style can, in fact, encompass many different looks. As well as the archetypal English cottage style, with its associated rose prints, comfortable furnishings and essential clutter, there are the more colourful styles of the rural Mediterranean where the heat of the summer and the different qualities of the light has inspired a more colourful and simpler country style. These looks, and others, reflect the local landscape, materials and climate. Our contemporary interpretation of country style is not dictated by our surroundings or limited to locally available materials. It can therefore be much more eclectic and highly individual, because we can pick and choose the elements we use according to the decorative country styles we find most appealing.

One of the hallmarks of the country-style home, whatever its influence, is the use of hand-crafted accessories. These can help turn a characterless house into a personalized home, and they can be tremendously rewarding to make. Crafts, such as embroidery and quilt-making, are time-consuming, but this is part of their appeal. The care and attention that they demand date back to a time when people did not expect instant results, and when far more value was attached to personal items than in today's throwaway society.

Other accessories in the country-style home make use of the wealth of beautiful materials and objects that nature provides. As well as flowers and vegetables, we can harvest fruits, twigs, pebbles, eggs and feathers to use in a rich variety of ways. Displays can be as simple and spontaneous as a handful of freshly picked flowers placed in a jam jar, or a simple bowl of round, shiny pebbles; or they can be more carefully crafted, such as a celebratory wreath or garland. The fact that natural gifts are available free of charge makes them even harder to resist, and it would have been an important factor in times when the need for thrift was an essential part of daily survival. In parts of the world that have seasonal variation, materials such as plants and flowers offer the perfect opportunity to create ever-changing looks and bring different colours into the home on a temporary basis.

The kitchen has always been the heart of the country home, a place of activity and bustle where the warmth of the stove, the mouth-watering aromas of home-cooked food, and a relaxed welcome reign supreme. The country kitchen is the place to prepare treats that can be enjoyed straight from the oven: freshly sliced bread that is still warm, wickedly indulgent cakes, and melt-in-the-mouth cookies to tempt the strictest of dieters.

The essence of a country home is that it is pleasing and comfortable for those who live there, and offers warmth and hospitality to visitors dropping by or for longer-term guests. Country crafts are relaxing and therapeutic and provide an opportunity to create your own country style. This book is full of ideas and inspiration for crafts, gifts and recipes – different textures, fabrics, ingredients, decorative details and colours – to help you settle on your own country style.

*Simple posies of seasonal flowers make beautiful centrepieces for almost any focal point (above right). Use traditional crafts such as wirework to create stylish kitchen accessories, like this attractive wire basket and wall hanger (right).*

# Country Style

Inspired by nature, country style transcends time and appeals to people of all ages. With fabrics woven from natural fibres, and

colours inspired by natural pigments, it is an informal look that will always suggest comfort and homeliness.

As a style of interior design, the country look is enduringly popular. Although the rapidly changing fashions in home decor over recent decades have had their effects, the essential charm of the country remains the same: homes feel warm, welcoming and informal; colours and designs are mixed and matched to create an impression of spontaneity, and furniture and accessories appear both decorative and functional. The style is, essentially, based on a pastoral idyll that we associate with a happier, simpler, slower way of life. A style that originally would have resulted from limited resources and the demands of rural life has become a fashion choice, as we strive to recreate a cosy country atmosphere in our comfortable modern homes.

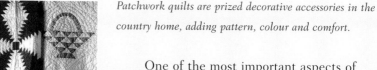

*Patchwork quilts are prized decorative accessories in the country home, adding pattern, colour and comfort.*

One of the most important aspects of country style is the use of colour. Traditionally, the colour palette was based on natural pigments and dyes, often made from local clays and plant material. As a result, colours were often deep-toned and smudgy. The introduction of manufactured paint meant that lighter tones were used, although colours still reflected the natural world, from blue-greens and mossy shades to poppy reds. Geographical variations are still seen: in the pale light of northern climates, colours are pastel and muted; in the Mediterranean and Mexico, they become brighter and more vibrant. Neutral tones are a universal

*Painted shelves and rustic earthenware look perfect in the kitchen.*

*Mix and match pretty yet practical items for a fresh, welcoming look.*

*Natural fibres and familiar motifs add cosiness to hard surfaces.*

*Plain colour schemes keep a room looking uncluttered.*

feature. The colours of traditional building materials, such as stone, wood and straw, now provide inspiration for a look that feels both natural and harmonious.

Traditional country fabrics would also have been natural, and even today's manufactured linens, cottons and wools have a homespun quality that is perfect for the country look. Plain fabrics, gingham, checks, stripes, spots and other geometric designs all feature, and the overall effect is crisp, fresh and cheerful. Motifs recur, on fabrics as well as walls, furniture and accessories: again, these are based on the natural world, with flowers such

as roses, foliage and animals all making a regular appearance. The objects depicted are simple, familiar and comforting, reinforcing the impression of cosy nostalgia.

Country-style paint finishes are produced by stippling, sponging, and ragging, which are original techniques that would have been used to add colour, texture and a decoration to a home in the most inexpensive way possible. Other techniques used today, such as the antiquing and distressing of furniture, are attempts to reproduce the patina of old painted furniture after generations of use.

# Plain & Simple Hues

*Although we are no longer dependent on colours derived from local materials, the natural environment still provides a wealth of inspiration for exciting, country-style colour schemes.*

COLOUR IS ONE OF the quickest and most powerful ways of stamping the country look on your home, and it is worth giving careful thought to the shades used for floors, ceilings and fabrics, as well as walls. Colour can influence the apparent size and temperature of a room, so your choice may depend on whether you wish the room to feel calm and restful, or warm and cheerful. Whether you opt for traditional pigments such as creams, earthy browns, stone colours and terracotta, or take inspiration from the more cheerful palette of the sky, leaves and flowers, colours should always look natural. This is not the style for neon primaries. If you decide to use a pattern, stick to a maximum of two colours in a regular design. Alternatively, muted cream or pastel tones used on the walls, with more vibrant trimmings, furniture and accessories, would give any home a fresh, country look.

RIGHT: Pistachio green is a favourite country colour that is easy to live with. The contrasting ribbon-trimmed shelf edging adds a delightful touch to this useful dresser.

## Gingham Wall

*The yellow gingham-effect on this wall*
*gives a bright, sunny feel to the room.*
*Paint the whole room, or use it for*
*a feature wall, or half walls.*

### MATERIALS

| | |
|---|---|
| *emulsion (latex) in* | *plumb line* |
| *off-white and yellow* | *chalk* |
| *2 paint rollers* | *spirit rule* |
| *measuring tape* | *pencil* |
| *craft knife* | |

1 Using a roller, apply two coats of off-white emulsion (latex) to a well-prepared wall. Allow to dry thoroughly between each coat.

2 Measure the width of the second roller and mark into thirds. Using a craft knife, cut out the middle section.

3 Find the mid-point of the wall and mark it using a chalked plumb line. Measure half the width of the cut roller from here and mark the wall at this point too. Measure and mark one-third of the width of the roller from this point and then a full width and mark. Repeat on the other side.

4 Load the roller with yellow paint and paint the middle section. Then, leaving the marked one-third blank, roll between the two chalk lines of the full width. Repeat on the other side. Leave another one-third space and mark the next full width on each side and paint. Complete the wall or room. Allow to dry.

5 Mark horizontal stripes using a spirit rule. Rule a true horizontal as near to the top of the wall as possible. Measure down as you measured across, and mark the horizontals in pencil, and paint them in yellow too.

BELOW: Country colours mirror the tones of the great outdoors, bringing a fresh, relaxing feel into our daily lives. Purples and lilacs were rarely seen in country homes, because they were extremely difficult colours to extract from plants. This made them so expensive that they eventually became associated with royalty.

LEFT: Mediterranean colours are warmer in tone and used in a less restrained way than in those countries with cooler climates. The distressed paint effect of these shutters is easy to create and adds to the country look.

# Neutral Tones

*The neutral palette incorporates a vast range of hues, from charcoal black to fresh white,*
*with all the shades of grey, beige and cream in between.*

WEATHERED WOOD, old stone, rich earth and silver bark are just a few of the materials that have inspired paint colours for the country home. These colours and materials are easy to live with. Paint, flooring, fabrics, furniture, accessories and trims in these soft tones help to create a harmonious atmosphere. If you can include natural materials such as wood and stone, so much the better. Neutral colours also accentuate materials with different textures, such as fibre matting and patterned weaves. Keep the look fresh by adding creams and paler tones in spring and summer, and by throwing in more textures and warm earthy shades for winter. Never worry about adding tone on tone: with neutrals this contributes to the depth of the overall look.

ABOVE: Creams and palest greys, teamed with a touch of white, make an elegant table setting.

RIGHT: Cream and white can work well together: the result is light, airy and calming.

## String-trimmed Tablecloth

*The texture of hessian (burlap) looks fantastic when teamed with other natural tones. Best of all, it is inexpensive and so is the perfect solution for long tablecloths. This cloth has been edged in upholsterer's webbing with a string decoration.*

### MATERIALS

| | |
|---|---|
| 2m/2½yd hessian (burlap) | 8m/8¾yd upholsterer's webbing |
| brown household string | sewing kit |

1 Cut the hessian to the required size. Turn in, press and stitch a double hem all around.

2 Pin, then stitch the webbing around the hem.

3 Arrange the string on top of the webbing in a twisting design. Pin and hand-stitch in place using slip stitch.

RIGHT: The rich tones of an antique polished wooden chair and the wooden floor make perfect partners, set off by the pure white of the sheer curtains.

ABOVE: Natural tones lend a co-ordinated look to disparate styles. These cushions range from the elegant rouleau-fastened and smart-buttoned to the fun fringed and bobbled, yet together they look cohesive and inviting. This is a great advantage if you want to update a scheme over the years, but you are reluctant to throw out perfectly good old favourites. Enhance the effect by mixing paler and deeper tones of neutral.

# Prints & Weaves

*Add interest to any country-style room with the creative use of natural fabrics, such as cottons, linens and wools, woven and printed in classic designs.*

PLAIN COLOURS ARE not the only hallmark of the country look. Timeless patterns, such as tartans, gingham, stripes, spots and simple geometric designs, have an informal charm that enliven a country-style room, without making it appear elaborate or cluttered. Floral and sprig designs also feature in many country homes, either as patterns in their own right, or woven or printed against a background of other designs, such as checks or stripes.

Again, the beauty of country style is the ease with which different prints and weaves can be mixed and matched; checks can be combined with stripes, for example, perhaps in complementary colours. Even the checked or striped dishtowel occasionally features as an accessory. Traditionally, country dwellers used whatever materials were to hand, and with creative skills transformed them into tablecloths, quilts, curtains, blinds and even clothes.

RIGHT: "New" furnishings can be made by recycling old and worn clothes and textiles.

TOP: Small-scale florals are a good choice for furnishings for small rooms, or to add accent colours to larger and more blousy floral designs, such as for decorative details on cushions, or as part of a patchwork quilt design.

ABOVE: Lots of styles of fabric work well in the country home. Checks and ginghams always work well together provided the colours are complementary, or the scale of the check is varied if the same colour scheme is used.

## Country-style Seat Cover

*Frilled seat covers have an enduring charm that looks good in country-style homes.*
*Made in stripes and gingham fabric, these are pretty and unfussy.*

### MATERIALS

| | |
|---|---|
| paper for template | piping cord |
| fabric (see step 1 for quantities) | 1m/1yd tape for ties |
| | sewing kit |

1 Make a paper template of the chair seat, then use this as a pattern to cut out the fabric, adding an extra 1.5cm/⅝in all around for seam allowances. Cut one from fabric.

2 To make the piping, cut the piping cord 5cm/2in longer than the circumference of the seat. Cut a 2.5cm/1in strip of fabric on the bias the same length. Centre the cord on the wrong side of the fabric, fold the fabric around the cord. Pin, tack (baste) and stitch, leaving the ends free.

3 With raw edges aligned, pin and tack (baste) the piping all around the chair seat, on the right side of the fabric. Unravel the cord ends, trim and twist together. Overlap the piping ends, turning in the short end that will show on the cushion cover. Stitch in place.

4 For the frill, cut a piece of fabric twice the circumference of the seat and 10cm/4in wide. Turn in, press and stitch a hem on one long and two short sides. Make a line of running stitches 5mm/¼in from the long raw edge, then gather up the stitches to fit around the front and sides.

5 Aligning raw edges, place the frill right side down on top of the piping. Pin and stitch in place.

6 Cut the tape in half. Find the centre of each length of tape. Fit the chair cover over the chair seat and align the tape with the position of the chair legs. Pin and stitch.

# Simple Motifs

*Bring decorative interest to walls, floors, furniture and furnishings using familiar motifs that immediately bring a country feel to any interior.*

EVERYDAY MOTIFS OFTEN TEND to recur in wallpaper and fabric designs. Flowers, foliage and animals are among the favourites, and these images have instant appeal because they bring the comforting familiarity of the natural world into the home. The subjects depicted should always be instantly recognizable, and some may even have childhood connotations. Images might also be chosen because they have a strong artistic appeal: roosters, for example, offer plenty of scope for introducing flamboyant colours, and wild birds enable a designer to incorporate interesting, quirky shapes.

Different motifs lend themselves to particular crafts or methods of reproduction. Suitable motifs for appliqué, embroidery, tapestry and découpage projects would be simple designs, such as the triangular shapes of hens; the smooth lines of fish; fruits, such as apples, pears, strawberries and plums; and plain leaf shapes. Cross-stitch can be used to reproduce almost any motif successfully, and like stamping and stencilling paint techniques, can be used for both simple and detailed images.

ABOVE: Bold and colourful motifs add charm to any soft furnishing item. Checked fabric adds to the country style.

RIGHT: You could personalize a plain item of painted wooden furniture by adding an individual painted motif. If you are not confident enough to paint the motif freehand, trace a pre-printed design, scaling it up or down as required.

ABOVE: Even designs cut from paper can make temporary decorations for seasonal ornaments.

BELOW: A leaf border painted directly on to a stripped wooden floor brings decorative interest in the country tradition. The border should be painted on to the stripped floor using floor paint. Once completely dry, the whole floor should be painted with two to three coats of non-yellowing floor varnish. Allow the floor to dry and lightly sand it between coats.

## Rooster Cushion

*Flamboyant farmyard roosters are a favourite folk motif the world over. Set in a gingham cushion, they make a classic yet fun country accessory. Any image can be fixed on to fabric using a photocopied image and a proprietary image maker distributed by home dye manufacturers.*

### MATERIALS

rooster image

spray mount adhesive

sheet of white paper

30cm/12in square

50cm/18in calico

sewing kit

tube of image maker

(Dylon)

40cm/16in square

gingham

38cm/15in square

cushion pad

1 Photocopy a rooster image five times and cut out roughly. Spray mount the images on the white paper.

2 Cut a 30cm/12in square of calico and, following the instructions on the image maker product, transfer the photocopied roosters on to the calico.

3 Press under a small hem all around the rooster fabric. Centre on the gingham fabric, then stitch in place.

4 For the cushion back, cut two calico pieces, 40 x 30cm/ 16 x 12 in. Stitch a hem on one long edge of each.

5 Place the cushion front right side up on a flat surface, then place the two calico backing pieces right side down on top, so that the long raw edges align with the top and bottom of the gingham raw edges and the hems overlap in the middle. Pin and stitch all around. Turn right side out and insert the cushion pad.

# Country Finishes

*Bring colour and decoration to everyday furniture and add interest to bare walls using painted, stamped and applied finishes.*

OVER THE YEARS, country style has come to include a whole range of finishes that can be applied to a variety of surfaces around the home. Traditionally, the walls would have been washed, stippled, sponged and stamped; and furniture was painted, or decorated with découpage, lending endless different looks to home interiors. Sometimes, layer upon layer of finish applied over the years meant that an item formed a patina of its own; this certainly was the case with painted furniture, which would suffer knocks and wear, inadvertently revealing the colour of a previous layer.

The rich look of aged furniture has become so appealing that we even contrive to reproduce it today by painting on successive coats of different colours, then rubbing back the top layers to manufacture wear and tear on edges and corners. Although items for decoration can

be bought inexpensively from junk stores and auctions, it is important to remember that old should not mean tatty and flimsy. The item needs to be fairly robust as once it's decorated it will feature as a practical item of furniture in your home.

FAR LEFT: Spongeware is a popular earthenware paint decoration that gives a soft mottled effect to pottery, walls, floors and even fabric.

ABOVE: Walls can be stamped and painted to give the effect of wall-paper. The preparation takes time, but the results are worthwhile.

LEFT & BELOW: Découpage is a simple way to decorate furniture with elaborate motifs, even if you don't think of yourself as artistic. Images, such as these fish and chicks, are very carefully cut from magazines, books or prints and glued on to the pre-painted surface of the furniture. Once dry, the whole piece of furniture is coated with several thin coats of non-yellowing acrylic matt varnish, allowing each to dry thoroughly between applications, until the surface is perfectly smooth and the découpage looks as if it has been handpainted in place.

## Flowerpot Frieze

*This delightful 1950s frieze is made up of a combination of collage and paint stamping. It offers a charming way to use up wallpaper and giftwrap scraps. This effect is stamped and painted directly on to the wall. The stripes are painted with a fine paintbrush, then the flowers are stamped in place.*

### MATERIALS

| | |
|---|---|
| *wallpaper or giftwrap scraps* | *fine artist's paintbrush* |
| *scissors* | *large and small daisy rubber stamps* |
| *PVA (white) glue* | *stamp inkpads in a* |
| *green acrylic paint* | *variety of colours* |

1 Draw flowerpot shapes on wallpaper or giftwrap scraps and cut them out. Cut scalloped strips of paper and glue them in place along the top of each flowerpot, using PVA (white) glue. Allow to dry. Glue the flowerpots on to the wall at evenly-spaced intervals.

2 Using acrylic paint and a fine paintbrush, paint green stems growing out of each pot. Leave the paint to dry.

3 Ink the daisy stamps, using the lighter coloured inks first. If you want contrasting centres, remove the main colour from the daisy centre using a cotton wool bud (swab). Dab on the second colour using a fresh bud. Test the stamp on a sheet of scrap paper to remove any excess ink, then print on the wall at the ends of some of the stems.

4 Clean the stamps, then re-ink with the darker colours and print as before.

# Country Crafts

Exquisite quilts and pretty samplers are

delightfully decorative. Pressing flowers,

and printing with fruits are much

simpler crafts, but whichever you

choose, you will produce perfect

accessories for your home.

Handicrafts have always had an important place in the country home. Traditionally, this was often a case of necessity; if you needed an item such as a quilt, the best solution was to make one. Today, planning a craft project, working on it and producing something that is truly unique is still highly rewarding. A home filled with hand-crafted furnishings and decorations immediately expresses the personality of the family that lives there.

Traditional sewing crafts, such as patchwork quilt-making, appliqué and the stitching of rag rugs, have become true hallmarks of country style. Although the need to make good use of every scrap of fabric clearly played a part in their development, people would also have derived great satisfaction from the production of beautiful, intricately crafted pieces. The art of patchwork quilting

*Small-scale cross-stitch designs add a colourful theme to everyday table linen.*

became especially popular in 19th-century America, when the ready availability of manufactured prints brought the craft within the reach of most families. As well as bedcovers, quilts were also used as door and window covers, and floor mats. They were even used as currency to pay bills. Social gatherings called "quilting bees" were held, at which women would gather to quilt the patchwork tops that they had usually prepared beforehand.

Another craft skill, embroidery, dates back centuries, to a time when young girls were expected to create samplers as part of their education. The exercise taught a wide range of needlecraft skills – essential requirements when most household linen and clothing were made at home.

*Photocopied transfer motifs lend wit to a modern patchwork cushion.*

*Pressed flowers add interest to church candles.*

*Cross stitch can be used to add exquisite decorative detail to many household items, such as this pillowcase and sheet.*

*Traditional metal and wirework are decorative and functional crafts that add individuality to the kitchen.*

Other crafts, such as tinwork and wirework, also made use of recycled materials. Punched and painted tin has been especially associated with Hispanic folk art, such as that of New Mexico, while wirework has its origins in central Europe, and is over 400 years old. At the height of the craft's popularity, thousands of people were employed as wireworkers across Europe and America, fashioning a range of household objects, from fruit bowls to lampshades on a small scale, and wirework arches and furniture for the garden on a grander scale.

The key to the appeal of many country crafts is their strong link with the natural environment. The popular Victorian art of flower-pressing, for example, is a way of preserving a beautiful object and treasuring memories of a special walk or outing. Fruits and vegetables, too, can be used both as an inspiration for craft projects and as a tool to create them: people have been cutting shapes in potatoes to print patterns at kindergarten for generations, and fruits with attractive shapes can simply be cut in half to make a stamp.

# Tactile Textiles

*Design your own textiles the traditional country way, working simple patchwork quilts or using appliqué to add motifs and interest to the plainest of fabrics.*

PLAIN, WOODEN FLOORS and furniture can be hard and appear austere, and textile furnishings, such as rugs and cushions help to soften the overall effect. Traditional sewing crafts can be used to decorate a wide range of soft furnishings, such as quilts, cushions, table linens, throws, bedcovers and floor coverings.

Pretty patchwork quilts immediately lend country style to any bedroom. If you are a beginner and would like to make your own quilt, start with a simple one-patch quilt, using large patches that can be sewn together quickly. The trick is to make sure all the patches are accurately cut and stitched to keep the pieces, and therefore the finished quilt, square. The choice of fabric will give the quilt

LEFT: Shirting in fine cotton can be made up into wonderful quilts, with stripes and plains juxtaposed to create large-scale light and dark patterns.

RIGHT: Rag rugs were made from recycled household fabrics and clothes.

its style. Soft florals will create an authentic Victorian feel, while a more contemporary look requires plain fabrics or geometric patterns in brighter colours.

Appliqué, the craft of applying pictorial fabric shapes to an item of soft furnishing, has a charm all its own. A single motif will add focal interest to any plain item, and a

motif repeated all over the fabric is perfect for unique furnishings. To add texture at floor level, you might try the 200-year-old craft of rag rug-making, or one of the other traditional rug-making techniques, such as hand-hooking, which uses a hook to work fabric or yarn into exquisite, highly individual designs.

## One-patch Quilt

*A patchwork quilt is one of the most important icons of country style, and a one-patch quilt is quick and easy to make with a sewing machine.*

### MATERIALS

*For a small throw: a piece of cardboard 19cm/7½in square 1m/1yd each of two cotton fabrics sewing kit sharp dressmaker's scissors*

*2m/2yd medium-weight wadding (batting) brushed cotton single bed sheet 50cm/18in contrast fabric for the binding*

1 Using the cardboard square as a template, on the wrong side of each fabric, draw 27 squares. Accurately cut each out.

2 Machine-stitch the squares right sides together in rows of nine, alternating the fabrics. With right sides together and matching the seams, tack (baste), then stitch the rows. Press the seams open.

3 Arrange the wadding on a flat surface and place the patchwork right side up on top. Pin the layers together, then trim any excess wadding.

4 Fold the sheet in half and mark the middle of each side with a pin. Repeat with the patchwork. Spread the sheet on a flat surface and place the patchwork right side up on top. Align the pins, then, making sure both layers are flat, baste the layers together. Trim the edges of the sheet to the same size as the quilt. Tack around the edge, then stitch in place.

5 Measure around the quilt, then cut enough 7.5cm/3in-wide strips of contrast fabric to make the binding. Cut one strip for each side, allowing 5cm/2in for turnings.

6 With right sides together, stitch one strip along one side of the quilt. Fold the edging to the back of the quilt, fold in a small hem, then stitch in place. Repeat on the other side of the quilt. Trim any excess edging at each end.

7 Repeat with the top and bottom edging, enclosing the raw ends of the side edges. Finally, turn in and stitch the corners using slip stitch.

## Appliqué Blanket

*This delightful bird makes a charming decoration for a small blanket. Worked in appliqué, it is decorated with brightly-coloured embroidery.*

### MATERIALS

*pencil and paper sewing kit fusible webbing scraps of coloured blanket or thick felt*

*iron wool blanket sewing machine assorted embroidery threads*

1 Draw a simple bird shape to the required size. Trace the shapes on to the paper side of the fusible webbing, leaving space between each tracing. Cut out the shapes leaving a small margin around each.

2 Position each fusible webbing shape on the wrong side of your choice of fabric scraps. Fuse in place with an iron, following the manufacturer's instructions. Accurately cut out each shape on the traced line.

3 Position each shape on the right side of the blanket. Fuse in place. Zig zag stitch around the outlines, then add the legs and hand embroider any details.

# Easy Embroidery

*Simple embroidered motifs bring a delightful country feel to household linens and accessories,
and the skills are not difficult to master.*

THERE IS SOMETHING immensely satisfying about transforming a plain textile into an item of beauty with the addition of some tiny stitching. The range of household items that can be decorated in such a way is vast: tablecloths, napkins, cushion covers and bed linens can all be personalized, and embroidered pictures look impressive when carefully framed.

Cross stitch is immensely popular, and offers the opportunity and challenge of producing a creative piece of work with just one stitch. For the beginner, there is a huge variety of patterns to choose from, and as you become more advanced, you can create your own designs from scratch. There are also many other quick and easy embroidery stitches: these include straight, blanket, chain, running and back stitches, as well as French knots.

LEFT: An embroidered band turns a cake into a special occasion treat.

RIGHT: Use embroidery to add stylish decoration to your cottons and linens. Using just one colour thread on a plain colour creates a dramatic effect.

28

## Beaded Cover

*Plain and simple, this beaded cover is a quick and easy version of the intricate crochet variety traditionally used to protect food and drink from flying insects.*

### MATERIALS

| | |
|---|---|
| paper | 50cm/½yd gingham |
| sewing kit | fabric bias binding |
| 25cm/¼yd white net | eight large ceramic |
| (tulle) | beads |
| sewing machine | |

1 Draw a circular template on to paper and cut out. Fold the net in half to make a double thickness and pin the paper pattern on to it. Stitch around the edge of the paper and cut away any excess net.

2 Stitch one edge of the bias binding around the net, with the paper still in place, then pull the paper away.

3 Fold the bias to the other side and stitch into place.

4 Stitch the beads to the cover at equal intervals using strong double thread.

## Cross-stitch Jam Pot Covers

*Pretty woodland strawberries make delightful decorative tops for home-made jams and jellies. They would make the perfect complement to the beaded cover, and look very attractive displayed on open shelves in the country-style kitchen.*

### MATERIALS

| | |
|---|---|
| *For one cover:* | Anchor stranded |
| 32 count cream linen, | cotton, 1 skein of each |
| 20cm/8in square | of the following |
| strawberry stitching | colours: |
| chart (see page 64) | 862 dark green, |
| masking tape | 266 olive green, |
| small embroidery hoop | 243 bright green, |
| size 24 or 26 tapestry | 9046 bright red, |
| needle | 13 dull red, |
| elastic bands | 11 deep pink |
| natural raffia or string | 907 ochre. |

1 Fold the linen in half in each direction to find the centre and tack (baste) along the folds. Bind the edges with masking tape and fit into the embroidery hoop.

2 Starting at the centre and using two strands of cotton over two threads of linen, cross stitch the design from the strawberry stitching chart. Then work the back-stitch details using two strands of cotton: use 907 for the seeds and 266 for the stems. Remove the embroidery from the hoop, remove the masking tape and press carefully, embroidery-side down, on a towel.

3 Fray the edges of the linen by pulling out one thread at a time. Place the cover on the jam pot and secure with an elastic band covered with raffia or string.

# Tincraft & Wirework

*Tin and wire are two industrial materials that have been used creatively on a domestic scale for hundreds of years. With skill these materials can be transformed into decorative and beautiful objects.*

ABOVE: This punched metal bathroom cabinet is based on those of the American settlers, who produced a wide range of household objects and decorated them with punched patterns. Draw a design on to paper, tape it to one side of the metal foil, then punch the design using a hammer and sharp object, such as a nail. Attach it to the wooden cabinet with glue.

TRANSFORMING A MATERIAL like tin into beautiful objects for the country home dates back to 18th-century America, when people discovered a way to roll sheet metal. This new material could be fixed in panels on to pie safes, cut into decorative shapes, or turned into more practical items such as wall sconces, lanterns, cookie cutters and cake tins (pans). Once these items had been made, the Pennsylvanian Dutch could not resist decorating them. The decorations generally involved punching small holes into the metal using a hammer and a sharp object such as a large nail. The outlines produced were of typical country icons, such as leaves and flowers, hearts and birds. Although punching rolled metal was hard and sometimes dangerous work, the modern aluminium foils available in craft shops are easy to work and can be punched with a hammer and nail, and the lighter-weight foils can be indented using dried-out ballpoint pens.

Wirework is another traditional country craft that is easy to learn and looks effective. Since wire is available in so many thicknesses and with different coatings for indoor or outdoor purposes it has a number of uses. Bent into shapes, such as hearts and flowers, or even for Christmas decorations, thin wire can be used purely decoratively, and items can be made with fine details. Thicker wire can be made up into a range of strong and useful items, such as wire hanging baskets, trivets to protect wooden surfaces from hot plates, delicate napkin rings, and even bowls and plates. Look for different gauges of wire and different colours, and experiment with various combinations.

## Decorative Birds

*Inspired by European folk-art motifs, these foil birds make pretty ornaments for kitchen dressers.*

### MATERIALS

| | |
|---|---|
| paper | protective pad |
| pencil | dried-out ballpoint pen |
| scissors | dressmaker's tracing |
| 0.1mm/¹⁄₂₅₀ in | wheel |
| aluminium foil | 6mm/¹⁄₄ in hole punch |
| adhesive tape | |

1 Draw a simple bird template on paper and cut it out, then secure to aluminium foil with adhesive tape. Place the foil on a protective pad and draw around the shape using the dried-out ballpoint pen.

2 Remove the template. Use the dried-out ballpoint pen to draw in the head, beak, eye and large dots on the wing and neck of each bird. Use the dressmaker's wheel to mark the dotted lines. Use the scissors to cut out the bird.

3 Use the larger hole punch to make a hole for the eye.

## Window Box Edging

*This pretty repeating heart pattern can be used to edge a window box or flower pot. Made with galvanized wire, it is ideal for the garden.*

### MATERIALS

1.6mm/¹⁄₁₂ in
galvanized wire
tape measure
wire cutters
flat-nosed pliers

1 Cut a 43cm/17in length of galvanized wire and bend it in half. Holding the centre with pliers twist the two ends around each other twice, leaving a small loop at the centre point. This is the centre of the small heart.

2 Bend the two tails below the loop and cross them to form a small heart shape. Hold the shape with pliers and twist the wire at the crossing point three times.

3 Bend the free ends out and down. Bend a 48cm/19in length of wire into a larger heart. Fit it around the smaller heart and twist the ends around the ends of the smaller heart. Trim the ends.

BELOW: In hot weather, protect food from flies and other insects with a food safe made from a wire frame covered with gauze fabric.

# Pressed Flowers

*With their passion for memorabilia, the Victorians were immensely fond of pressing flowers,*
*and the craft adds a pretty, natural look to today's country-style home.*

DELICATE PRESSED FLOWERS and leaves can be used to decorate a variety of home accessories. Candles, trays, lampshades, picture frames and trinket boxes can all be given a fresh look.

It is best to use garden flowers because many rare wild flowers, such as cowslips, are protected to ensure they mature fully and produce seed. Simple-shaped flat flowers, such as primroses, pansies and violets, press best because they dry out very quickly. More fleshy, complex flowers, such as roses or peonies, which are many-petalled, are inclined to retain moisture and may become mildewed. However, you can always take these flowers apart and press individual petals. For the best results, pick the flowers on a dry morning when the dew has dried, but before the blooms can be scorched by the hot sun. To press flowers, petals or leaves, place good specimens between sheets of absorbent tissues or kitchen paper under a pile of heavy books. After about a week, check them. If they are dry and papery, they are ready to be used; if not, replace them for a few more days.

LEFT: Pressed flowers can be used unconventionally to decorate walls. Fix them in place using PVA (white) glue. Allow to dry. Paint on two coats of matt acrylic varnish, allowing each layer to dry between coats.

ABOVE: Petals can be used to decorate candles. If you make your own, press petals into the sides as the hot wax fills the mould, or you could melt some wax and use it to adhere pressed petals to the outside of the candle.

## Nature Notebook

*Make a unique album from hand-made paper, then decorate it with pressed flowers, collected from the hedgerows on a summer's day. Fill it with photographs of friends and family, taken on special days in the country.*

### MATERIALS

| | |
|---|---|
| *craft knife* | *fine artist's paintbrush* |
| *metal ruler* | *PVA (white) glue* |
| *cutting mat* | *hand-made papers for* |
| *thick hand-made paper* | *the pages* |
| *for the cover* | *large bulldog clip* |
| *silicone paper* | *hole punch and* |
| *fine paper* | *hammer* |
| *glue stick* | *darning needle* |
| *selection of pressed* | *raffia* |
| *flowers to decorate* | *twine* |

BELOW: Pressed violas and daisy petals make a delightful decoration for a chequerboard tray. First paint the tray blue and allow to dry completely. Next, draw on the chequerboard and paint in the squares. Once the paint is fully dry, fix the pressed flowers and petals in place using PVA (white) glue. Allow the glue to dry, then finish with two coats of matt acrylic varnish, leaving each coat to dry completely before applying the next.

1 For the cover, using a craft knife and metal ruler, and working on a cutting mat, cut a piece of thick hand-made paper twice as long as the desired page size. Fold it in half along the short edge and smooth the crease under a protective sheet of silicone paper. Tear the two short edges to give a ragged effect.

2 To decorate the front of the cover, tear a strip of fine paper and fix in position with the glue stick.

3 Arrange the pressed flowers on the strip of paper. Lift and apply a tiny dab of glue to the back of each.

4 Allow the glue to dry, then apply tiny dabs of glue to the back of the petals and press down gently.

5 For the inside pages, cut sheets of the fine paper to the desired page size. Cut or tear pages of the same size from a selection of hand-made papers.

6 Assemble the hand-made paper pages with a sheet of fine paper between each one. Place inside the cover and hold in place with a bulldog clip at the top.

7 Mark holes 2.5cm/1in from the spine, and 2.5cm/1in apart. Working on a surface that cannot be damaged, pierce with a hole punch and hammer.

8 Using a darning needle, thread a short length each of raffia and twine and stitch together through the first two holes at the top and bottom of the notebook, working over the spine. Knot the ends on the back of the book and trim neatly.

9 Thread the needle again with raffia only this time and back-stitch through the remaining holes. Repeat with the twine. Tie the ends neatly at the back of the notebook and trim.

# Country Prints

*Making your own prints from fruits, vegetables, flowers and leaves is great fun, and the finished results will add a creative and individual touch to your furnishings.*

STAMPS MADE FROM natural objects can be used to decorate a surprising number of items in the country-style home. Soft furnishings such as curtains, blinds and cushions; wooden furniture; accessories, such as trays, boxes and lamp bases; and even entire walls and floors can all be hand-printed in this way. As well as carving vegetables, such as potatoes, into interesting motifs, you can simply cut those fruits that are a pleasing shape in half, and use them as stamps. Alternatively use a rubber stamp or make a complex design from linoleum.

RIGHT: The calico of this cushion was printed using unripe apples and pears. They were cut in half, painted with fabric paint, and then used to print a design on the pre-washed calico. Once that was dry, the wiped fruit halves were used to print bronze fabric paint on top. Finally, a soft, broken line of black fabric pen was used to add definition. Another country print idea is to use flowers and leaves as masks, then stipple over them to leave the imprint of their outline. Whichever method you choose, it is a good idea to practise your design on a rough sheet of paper first, until you are happy with the overall effect.

## Sponge-printed Fruit Shelf Edging

*This quirky design is quick and easy to make and has a modern country feel.*

### MATERIALS

*13cm/5in strip of
unbleached, washed
and ironed
calico, the length of
the shelf
iron
pencil and scissors
fruit and leaf stamps*

*paintbrush
fabric paints in red,
yellow and green
6cm/2½in strip of
green print cotton, the
length of the shelf
sewing kit
spray fabric stiffener*

1 Press the length of calico and fold it concertina-style until the folds are approximately 13cm/5in wide.

2 Measure and mark 5cm/2in down each fold from the top long edge. Find the centre point along the bottom long edge. Draw lines joining up the side and centre bottom points and cut out. Open out the strip.

3 Print a leaf shape on to each side of a fruit. Stipple darker areas on the fruit and leaves with a paintbrush to give them a three-dimensional look. Allow to dry.

4 Fold the green print cotton in half along the long edge, wrong sides together, and press. Open out the fold. Turn in a 5mm/¼in seam allowance on one long edge. Press.

5 Place the green cotton on top of the printed fabric, right sides together and raw edges aligned. Stitch in place, using a 5mm/¼in seam allowance. Fold the green fabric along the pressed line, and slip-stitch the folded hem to the back of the seam.

6 Spray with fabric stiffener, then attach to the shelf using double-sided tape.

LEFT: Large American oak leaves have been used to print a design to decorate round boxes. Paint the boxes and lids pale grey and leave the paint to dry. Next, hold a leaf in place on the side of the box and over the rim of the lid. Stipple cream paint around the edge of the leaf. Move the leaf around the box and stipple again until the design is complete. Allow to dry. Remove the lid, align the leaf with the shape on the side and fill in the details under the rim.

# Country Gifts

Displays of flowers, fruits, leaves and herbs

bring the essence of each season's ambience

into the heart of our homes, enabling

us to enjoy all the colours,

textures and delicate perfumes

of nature all year round.

One way to celebrate a love of the countryside is to bring a little of it indoors. The natural world offers an inspirational supply of materials, such as flowers, twigs, stones, pebbles, fruits, eggs and feathers. There is an abundance of shapes, textures, colours and patterns in the fields and hedgerows, and the passing seasons provide endless possibilities for creating fresh and varied looks in the country home.

Twigs and stones or pebbles offer vast potential for creating original, organic works of art, but traditionally, rural households would have also had practical uses for these materials. Stones were of course essential for construction purposes as were twigs and branches, used in the making of thatched roofs, and wattle and daub walls. In addition, the branches of particular trees had specific functions: common hazel was used to weave baskets, wych elm was used to make chair seats, and rowan twigs were hung in the window to ward off evil spirits.

*Flowers make a delightful decoration on a gift ,wrapped with pressed flower paper.*

Other natural objects retain associations with certain times of year, and displaying these icons around the home can be extremely satisfying. Eggs are firmly linked with Easter, and a bowl of natural or painted eggs makes a wonderful centrepiece for the spring table. In the autumn, wheat sheaves and corn dollies make attractive wall hangings in the country kitchen. Decorations made from feathers can evoke both winter, when they would traditionally have come into their own in quilts to keep the family warm, and spring, with their associations with nest-building and new life.

A posy of fresh, seasonal flowers is another way of ringing the changes, satisfying the senses and bringing colour and beauty into the home. Flowers were particularly important to the Victorians and they developed a whole language of flowers. Each flower had a specific meaning,

*Decorated eggs are an attractive centrepiece for an Easter table.*

*Rosehips look exquisite when bound into a wild-looking wreath.*

*A heart-shaped container is filled with florist's dry foam, then covered with dried flower and seed heads to make an attractive arrangement.*

and a bouquet could be created to convey a range of emotions. Some traditional meanings remain today: snowdrops, for example, are still regarded as unlucky if brought into a house. The native British evergreens used on decorative winter wreaths have a symbolism of their own. In the Middle Ages, mistletoe was regarded as a magical plant, with powers as an aphrodisiac and fertility potion, and some people still consider bumper crops of holly berries to be a sign that hard weather is to come, despite more modern scientific explanations.

For the times when nature's store is less lush and bountiful, dried flowers and herbs can be used instead of fresh ones. As well as smelling exquisite, dried flowers, such as lavender, can also be put to practical use, whether it is to deter insects, freshen clothes or induce sleep. In addition, the fragrant blends of dried flowers and leaves mixed with oils and exotic spices known as pot pourris were not commonly made until the mid-18th century, although powdered dried petals had been used in the home since medieval times.

# Twigs & Pebbles

*Even the most unlikely countryside materials, such as sticks, stones, twigs and pebbles, can be turned into something beautiful for the home.*

STICKS AND STONES CAN be surprisingly attractive. While the leafy abundance of summer has an obvious beauty, twigs have a skeletal form that is almost sculptural. In spring, there is something magical about bringing in what looks like a few gnarled sticks, and then, during the course of a week, watching them burst into a froth of blossom. In autumn, twigs again have their day producing bright berries or fruit. This is a good time of year to harvest some exquisite twigs, complete with rosehips, and bring them indoors for weeks of enjoyment.

When it comes to collecting pebbles, if you make it into a game, even small children will love to be involved. Once collected and brought home, larger stones can be varnished or painted with ladybird or beetle designs and used as paperweights and doorstops, while bowls of smaller varnished pebbles in myriad shades can be used to make attractive decorations for the bathroom.

RIGHT: Twigs with buds and blossom make striking natural decorations.

## Willow & Feather Star

*Light and airy in appearance, this delicate-looking star is much more robust than it first appears.*

### MATERIALS

18 willow sticks about 40cm/16in long

raffia

about 40 female pheasant feathers

high-tack glue

1 Place three bundles of three willow sticks on a surface to form a triangle, and bind the corners with raffia. Make another triangle in the same way.

2 Arrange one triangle on top of the other to form a star, and bind it together at all the points where the triangles cross. Trim the ends of the sticks to neaten.

3 Using high-tack glue, stick some feathers to the inner star, wedging them between the sticks.

4 To finish off each point of the star, tie a pair of feathers into a v-shape using raffia, and glue in place.

RIGHT: Plain and inexpensive picture frames can be decorated with small sticks and stones using PVA (white) glue for an individual country look. Choose twigs with an interesting bark, use driftwood as shown here, or look out for twigs with lichen growing on them. Flat, round stones worn smooth by a stream make good choices, as do pebbles with bands or veins of different colours. A coat of varnish will keep them looking as bright as they did in the water.

LEFT: Beach pebbles and tiny pieces of driftwood make a quirky lampshade trimming. Choose a strong lampshade that has a punched lower edge, then bind this with raffia. Tie a piece of raffia around each pebble and stick together, adding a spot of PVA (white) glue to fix the raffia, then tie in position on the lampshade.

# Welcoming Garlands

*Seasonal garlands make beautiful decorations. We most commonly associate them with Christmas,*
*but there is no reason why they should be limited to winter.*

G ARLANDS MADE OF seasonal material gathered from the countryside make wonderful decorations for the home. They will generally last longer than fresh floral arrangements, although, since they are made of fresh material, few last more than a season, and some for little longer than a week. They will give pleasure for longer when they are made from dried material, or from fresh flowers that can be formed into a wreath, and then allowed to dry. Lavender is an excellent material to use. It is easier to work with when freshly picked, but will slowly dry out to give months of perfume. Grasses, too, will dry well, though it's worth remembering that if they are used while still green, they will turn yellow as they dry.

Although garlands are generally circular, there is no reason why they should not be different shapes. To make a heart or a star, simply make a circular wire base, then bend it into the shape that you want. Bind it with florist's tape before fixing on the material.

LEFT: This delicate but striking heart-shaped garland was made from buddleia branches, variegated ivy, autumn berries and a single white rose.

## Wild Barley Ring

*Search any patch of long grass in early summer, and you will find an*
*abundance of wild barley – you don't even need to be in the country.*

MATERIALS

2.5m/8ft garden wire
florist's tape
wild barley

1 Make a circle about 18cm/7in diameter using several thicknesses of garden wire, and bind all the way around using florist's tape.

2 Make bundles of six ears of barley, cutting the stems to about 5cm/2in, then bind together with florist's tape.

3 Bind the first bundle to the outside of the wire ring with florist's tape. Place the next bundle on the inside of the wire, overlapping the stems of the first, and bind in place. Continue until the ring is complete.

## Dogwood Heart

*In early spring, the countryside abounds with the young burgundy shoots of dogwood. Mature shrubs produce a mass of branches, a few of which can be pruned without affecting the overall shape of the shrub. Use the branches as soon as you can after cutting, while they are full of sap and still pliable, to make this charming decoration.*

### MATERIALS

*generous bundle of dogwood shoots (Cornus alba)*

*florist's reel wire secateurs (pruners) raffia*

1 Select two bundles of about five long shoots and very carefully bend each bundle into a large U-shape. Hold these shapes at right angles to each other to make a heart shape. Use the florist's wire to join the two shapes together where they cross. This can take a little patience because you will need to keep easing the bundles of dogwood gently into position.

2 Wire the bottom point of the heart. Trim any long ends with the secateurs. Build on the basic heart shape, thickening it up by adding more pliable, finer, shorter shoots at the top and fixing them in place with florist's wire.

3 Finish the decoration by binding all the joints with raffia.

LEFT: To make this heart, arrange 120 large lavender heads with 2.5cm/1in stems into bunches of six. Secure the bunches with florist's wire. Form a circle from a 112cm/44in length of garden wire by making a hook at each end. Bend the wire into a heart and then use florist's tape to bind the bunches in place. Tie a bunch of lavender with wire and raffia, attach to the bottom of the heart and secure with a bow.

# Pretty Posies

*Irresistible country flowers remind us of the passing seasons, offering new treats every week of the year.*
*Cut some to bring colour and perfume into the house.*

A BEAUTIFUL POSY OF flowers, freshly picked from the garden, is a charming addition to any room. A simple arrangement works best, so dispense with any artificial supports, such as florist's foam or chicken wire. Choose a straightforward container that is suited to the material, so the stems can fall naturally and do not appear contrived or forced. Simple vases, jugs (pitchers), glasses and even jam jars are all very much in keeping with the country look. When selecting flowers to grow, go for traditional varieties, such as roses, marigolds, love-in-the-mist, sweet peas, stocks, poppies and cornflowers, and try to avoid modern hybrids.

Ideally, flowers should be picked early in the day, before the morning dew has had a chance to dry, or late in the evening. If possible, place the stems in water for a few hours before transferring them to the container in which they will be displayed.

RIGHT: Richly perfumed and brightly coloured garden flowers sum up all that is beautiful about a country garden in the summer.

LEFT: The sweet scent of lily-of-the-valley set against vibrant emerald green leaves are a rare treat in spring. In folklore, they symbolize the return of hope as the days lengthen and the coldest nights are left behind.

## Herbal Tussie Mussie

*These delightful aromatic posies were originally carried by ladies in centuries past to overcome the 'bad odours' that were then commonplace – but that need not diminish their charm. This one is made from rosemary leaves, comfrey and chive flowers, all collected from a traditional country garden, and tied with a ribbon.*

### MATERIALS

| | |
|---|---|
| large bunch rosemary | bunch of comfrey |
| 5 chive flowers | secateurs (pruners) |
| green raffia | grosgrain ribbon |

1 Arrange a circle of rosemary around the five chive flowers and tie with raffia. Next, place a ring of comfrey around the rosemary and bind. Encircle the whole tussie mussie with a final ring of rosemary and tie firmly in place with raffia.

2 Trim all the stalks. Tie the posie with a length of blue grosgrain ribbon.

BELOW LEFT: Just a few carefully chosen cottage flowers bring life to a country home. Here, an anemone de Caen makes a centrepiece for a posy of primroses and auriculas, set off by the vibrant green of lady's mantle. Make them into a pleasing arrangement, then tie to secure, and place in a vase. Lady's mantle has delicate sprays of tiny flowers in summer, but when not in flower, the foliage is most attractive. The leaves will trap droplets of water, which catch the sun and sparkle, with the appearance of dew on a bright, fresh morning.

# Seasonal Icons

*Celebrate the changing seasons by bringing in the best flowers, foliage and found objects that nature can offer, to create the most appealing seasonal decorations.*

AN AWARENESS OF the seasons was traditionally vital for country survival to ensure that the harvest was brought in on time and the produce was preserved to last the winter through. Just as in the past, people still love to bring seasonal flowers, fruits and produce into their homes. They add colour, freshness, scent and interest to our homes. Over time, spring's blossoms, bulbs, eggs, feathers and nests; summer's roses and sunflowers; autumn's fruits, berries and pumpkins; and winter's holly and ivy gradually became symbols of the differing seasons. Nowadays the passing of the seasons and the extent of the harvest no longer have such a fundamental effect on our daily lives, but recognizing the changes in the season can bring additional cheer to our lives.

LEFT: This beautiful sleeping face makes an exquisite autumnal pumpkin decoration.
RIGHT: Sunflowers, lavender and citrus fruits are the epitome of a Mediterranean summer.

## Springtime Garland

*The combination of willow twigs and*
*eggshells make a delightful springtime wreath. To*
*simplify this project you could use a ready-formed*
*twig wreath and add your choice of decoration.*

### MATERIALS

| | |
|---|---|
| *willow twigs, soaked in* | *long, large-eyed* |
| *lukewarm water* | *needle* |
| *fine wire* | *wire-edged organza* |
| *artificial quails' eggs* | *ribbons* |

1 Bend a group of five or six long twigs into a circle and
secure in place with wire. Add smaller twigs to the
circle, intertwining the ends to make a firm structure.

2 Using a large needle, pierce a hole in each end of each
artificial egg and carefully feed fine wire through the
holes. Wire them to the front of the wreath.

3 Using a long needle, thread organza ribbon through the
wreath and tie it into bows or knots.

LEFT: The blue-green leaves of eucalyptus have a winter
feel to them, especially when teamed with seasonal
white flowers for winter. These beautiful hellebores are
perfect, but you could use white anemones if you prefer.
To make this candle arrangement, cut a florist's foam
ball in half and soak half in water. Discard the other half.
Push three candles of differing heights into the centre of
the foam. Cut sprigs of eucalyptus into pieces about
16cm/6in long and arrange them over the foam, pushing
the end of each sprig in to secure it. Cut the flower
stems to 12.5cm/5in and arrange at intervals between
the eucalyptus. Stand the foam in a complementary bowl
and use as a winter table arrangement.

# Decorative Drying

*There are plenty of fresh materials, other than flowers, that dry well, and some creative experimenting could produce stunning decorations and ornaments for the country home.*

THERE ARE MANY country materials that dry well, retaining their colour, and some, such as lavender, that keep their evocative perfume, too. Dried flowers and herbs combine well with spices and dried fruit peels to make beautifully fragranced pot pourris, and can also be made into lasting decorations for the home. The trick with dried flowers is to devise ways of using the most colourful or textured part – usually the seedhead or the flower.

Other natural materials that dry well include leaves, and even beans, which can be used to make interesting wreaths,

topiaries and pictures. A bowl of fresh fruits, some studded with cloves in attractive designs, then left to dry out, makes an appealing centrepiece for the kitchen or dining-room table.

Above: Bay leaves dry to a soft grey-green, while retaining their distinctive aroma.

ABOVE: These classic pomanders, made by studding cloves into fresh oranges, would once have been used to keep insects away from fabrics.

LEFT: These pomanders are made by studding cloves into foam balls, then gluing cardamom pods to the spaces left.

## Yarrow Topiary

*Yarrow (Achillea millefolium) dries beautifully, retaining its mellow old-gold tones. Each flower head provides a generous cushion of colour, making it very quick and easy to work with.*

### MATERIALS

florist's dry foam block
yellow container
bunch of
willow sticks about
45cm/18in long
secateurs (pruners)
raffia

florist's dry foam ball
18cm/7in diameter
3 bunches dried yarrow
(Achillea millefolium)
1 bunch love-in-the-mist (Nigella orientalis)
dried autumn leaves

1 Trim the foam block to fit tightly into the container. The top of it should finish about 1cm/½in below the rim of the container.

2 To make the stem of the topiary, cut the willow sticks to an even length. Bind them with two strands of raffia and fix into the foam block, pushing the sticks firmly into the container. Push the florist's foam ball firmly on to the other end of the sticks.

3 Cut the yarrow stems to about 2.5cm/1in and push them firmly into the foam ball, completely covering it and retaining the spherical shape.

4 Trim the love-in-the-mist stems to about 5cm/2in and add to the ball at regular intervals. Make sure the entire shape is covered and that no foam is visible.

5 Arrange a selection of dried autumn leaves to completely cover the foam in the container.

ABOVE: These quirky lavender trees were created by fixing a florist's dry foam ball on to a willow twig in much the same way as the yarrow topiary.

RIGHT: To make this dried bean heart, draw a heart shape on to the backing paper from a small picture frame. Squeeze a line of glue along the pencil line. Stick a neat line of mung beans to the glue. Add another line of beans to the inside of the first line, and continue until the shape is complete. Allow to dry. Cover the background with glue, then stick haricot (navy) beans over the surface to fill.

# The Kitchen

Irresistible aromas of cooking make the

country kitchen the heart of the country

home. This is where the whole family

can make mouth-watering

desserts, sweets and candies, as

well as delicious tea-time treats.

Warm and inviting, the kitchen is the heart of the home and the creative hub of the house. It very often opens out into the garden, so fresh fruit, vegetables, flowers and herbs can easily be brought in and transformed into delicious home-made dishes for the whole family. With its pure ingredients, country cooking is traditionally simple, wholesome and filling. Steaming stews, soups and pies, and roasted meats with fresh seasonal vegetables are typical fare, much of which could be cooked in advance. However, while these dishes are very satisfying, the pastries and puddings, sweets and treats are many people's favourites.

Baking is where the traditional country cook can really exercise skill. Summer fruits can be transformed into irresistible summer puddings, or teamed with meringue to make a pavlova. In autumn, apples and blackberries, pears and plums are shown off in pretty tarts and flans, tucked

*Dates decorated with nuts make a delicious treat for any time of the year.*

into pies topped with light pastries or crumbles, or wrapped into roly poly puddings. As winter approaches, delicious pecan pies and treacle tarts tempt the tastebuds, along with steamed jam puddings. Tea time is a particular treat, as most of the meal seems to indulge us with our favourites. Cakes large and small, biscuits and cookies, scones unashamedly lavished with clotted cream, crumpets dripping with butter, and waffles doused in syrup, are all on offer. Granted, we often must have a sandwich first – but they're traditionally made from bread cut as thinly as possible, with light fillings.

Skilled country cooks let the preparation of these treats become part of the welcome of the kitchen. They invite everyone to help with peeling and coring apples from the garden, ready to put into delicious pies or place

*Cookies make the perfect accompaniment to afternoon tea.*

*The smell of fresh bread baking is indescribably delicious.*

*Summer berries and freshly made scones are the perfect end to a picnic tea in the summer garden.*

decoratively on elegant tarts. At tea time, they leave the oven on, so when all the scones speedily disappear from the plate, another batch can be put in to bake. Scones turn out lighter and all the more delicious if they are made as quickly as possible with cold hands (so hold yours under cold water before putting them into the dough mixture). Since they need less than 10 minutes to bake, there won't be much waiting around, and

nobody's going to complain if the kitchen is warm and the company convivial.

Treats from the country kitchen hold such appeal that they always make welcome gifts. A prettily packaged box of cakes, cookies or candies makes a very special present for many occasions, whether it's to bring a little cheer to a friend, say thank you for a favour, or celebrate with relatives for the day or weekend.

# Afternoon Tea

*Wafer-thin sandwiches, scones, cakes and biscuits… the mid-afternoon break is packed with delicious treats. The ideal meal for children, it also provides adults with the perfect stopgap between lunch and dinner.*

AFTERNOON TEA MUST be the most civilized meal of the day for the whole family. The choice of treats on offer is guaranteed to delight, as people select as much or as little as they want. At the same time, the pick-and-mix quality of the meal conveniently sidesteps meal-time battles with the younger members of the family: with so many tempting treats on offer, most can be persuaded to eat at least one little healthy sandwich first.

Savouries usually include paper-thin sandwiches filled with thinly sliced cucumber or tomatoes, or with spreads such as fish pastes and vegetable extracts. There are toasted teacakes, crumpets and English muffins as an alternative. These are often followed by teabreads, scones and cream, home-made cakes or cookies, all served with refreshing cups of tea. For the younger generation, home-made lemonade, fruit cordials and ice-cold milkshakes are all popular.

RIGHT: Delightfully decorated with daisies, these home-made sponge cupcakes are topped with lemon icing.

## Scones

*Topped with clotted cream and jam, scones (biscuits) represent the essence of an English afternoon tea. The recipe makes 10–12.*

### INGREDIENTS

| | |
|---|---|
| 225g/8oz/2 cups plain (all-purpose) flour | 50g/2oz/4 tbsp butter |
| | 1 egg, beaten |
| 15ml/1 tbsp baking powder | 75ml/5 tbsp milk |
| | 1 beaten egg to glaze |

1 Preheat the oven to 220°C/425°F/Gas 7. Lightly butter a baking (cookie) sheet.

2 Sift the flour and baking powder together, then rub in the diced butter. Make a well in the centre of the flour mixture, add the egg and milk and mix to a soft dough, using a round-bladed knife.

3 Turn out the dough on to a lightly floured surface and knead until smooth. Roll out to 2cm/¾in thickness and use a 5cm/2in cutter to cut out the scones.

4 Transfer to the baking sheet, brush with beaten egg, then bake for about 8 minutes until risen and golden. Cool slightly on a wire rack before serving.

ABOVE: The airy sponge of a roulade make it a light and mouth-watering tea-time treat.

RIGHT: Even the most simple Victoria sponge cake takes on a celebratory feel when topped with a layer of pastel-coloured icing and decorated with beautiful garden roses. Use fresh roses that have been thoroughly washed.

# *Bread & Teabreads*

*A country kitchen filled with the irresistible aroma of home-baked, savoury bread flavoured with herbs*
*has a taste that is far superior to anything you can buy.*

Bread has moved on a long way from its humble beginnings as the standard daily fare of the poor. Every region of every country would have had its own special version and traditional loaves associated with different countries still exist. The Italians have transformed breads from a simple medium for soaking up sauces into a whole new art form. They are often flavoured with herbs, garlic, olives and sun-dried tomatoes. Many Mediterranean savoury breads include olive oil as an ingredient, which not only lends a delicious flavour to the bread, but helps it to keep longer, so you can make it the day before eating.

Teabreads, on the other hand, are a British speciality, while brownies and muffins are an American invention. There are dozens of traditional recipes and modern variations to choose from. Often enriched with fruit and nuts, these sweet cakes are an excellent choice for lunches, picnics, and afternoon tea.

RIGHT: Teabreads take many forms and include many different ingredients. They are usually sweet to taste.

## Warm Herby Bread

*This Italian-style bread, flavoured with basil, rosemary, olive oil and sun-dried tomatoes, is delicious served with fresh salads and sliced meats, such as Parma ham and salami. This recipe makes three loaves.*

### INGREDIENTS

1 tsp caster (superfine) sugar

900ml/1½ pints/ 3¾ cups warm water

1 tbsp dried yeast

1.5kg/3lb/12 cups strong plain (all-purpose) flour

1 tbsp fine salt

75ml/5 tbsp mixed chopped basil and

rosemary leaves

50g/2 oz/1 cup drained sun-dried tomatoes, roughly chopped

150ml/¼ pint/⅔ cup virgin olive oil

**To finish**

extra virgin olive oil

rosemary

sea salt flakes

1 Put the sugar into a small bowl and pour on 150ml/ ¼ pint/⅔ cup of the warm water, then sprinkle the yeast over the top. Leave in a warm place for 10–15 minutes until frothy.

2 Put the flour, salt, chopped basil and rosemary leaves and sun-dried tomatoes into a large bowl. Add the oil and yeast mixture, then mix in the remaining warm water.

3 As the mixture becomes stiffer, bring it together with your hands and mix to a soft but not sticky dough, adding a little extra water if needed.

4 Turn the dough out on to a lightly floured surface and knead for 5 minutes until smooth and elastic.

5 Put the dough back into the bowl, cover loosely with oiled clear film (plastic wrap) and put in a warm place for 30–40 minutes or until the dough has doubled in size. Knead again until smooth and elastic.

6 Cut the dough into three even-size pieces. Shape each one into an oval loaf about 18cm/7in long and arrange on an oiled baking sheet.

7 Preheat the oven to 220°C/425°F/Gas 7. Slash the top of each loaf with a knife in a criss-cross pattern. Loosely cover with a clean dish towel and leave in a warm place for 15–20 minutes until well-risen.

8 Brush the loaves with a little extra virgin olive oil and sprinkle with fresh rosemary leaves and sea salt flakes. Cook for about 25 minutes until golden brown. The bases should sound hollow when they are lightly tapped.

ABOVE: Teabreads made with fresh or freeze-dried strawberries or raspberries are light and taste moist and delicious.

# Old-fashioned Desserts

*Delicious country desserts make an irresistible finale to hearty meals and too often prove so tempting, that it's hard not to over-indulge.*

Howevver delicious the **main** course, it is always the desserts everyone looks forward to and nothing can beat the good old-fashioned variety: apple pies, mouth-watering blackberry and apple crumbles, tarts and soft steamed sponge puddings flavoured with gooey syrup or rich, indulgent chocolate. These are the country favourites, and many of the ingredients, such as fruits for fillings, and eggs for pastries and sponges, are still locally produced. These hearty desserts, packed with flavour, were designed to satisfy the sweetest tooth and more importantly, the healthiest of appetites, sharpened by a day working outdoors on the land.

These are desserts that prove almost irresistible as their sweet aroma rises when they are cut. Serve them with fresh cream, vanilla ice cream or real custard sauce and you will never yearn for shop-bought imitations again.

RIGHT: Bread and butter pudding is a hearty and filling dessert for winter. It has a number of variations and can be made with fresh cream and panettone.

# Date, Fig & Orange Pudding

*Warm up cold winter days with a comforting steamed pudding of rich dried fruits, enlivened with zesty orange. Serve it with a little whipped cream or custard.*
*The recipe serves six.*

## INGREDIENTS

*2 oranges*
*115g/4oz/scant 1 cup*
*pitted ready-to-eat*
*dried dates, chopped*
*115g/4oz/²⁄₃ cup*
*ready-to-eat dried figs,*
*chopped*
*30ml/2 tbsp Cointreau*
*or orange liqueur*
*(optional)*
*175g/6oz/¾ cup*
*unsalted (sweet) butter,*
*plus extra for greasing*

*175g/6oz/¼ cup soft*
*light brown sugar*
*3 eggs*
*75g/3oz/²⁄₃ cup self-*
*raising (self-rising)*
*wholemeal (whole-*
*wheat) flour*
*115g/4oz/1 cup*
*unbleached self-raising*
*flour*
*30ml/2tbsp golden*
*(light corn) syrup*
*(optional)*

1 Thinly pare a few pieces of rind from one orange, cut into fine strips and reserve for decoration. Grate the rind from the other orange and squeeze out the juice. Put the rind and juice into a pan. Add the dates and figs and orange liqueur. Cover and cook over a low heat for 8–10 minutes, or until the fruit is soft.

2 Leave the fruit to cool, then transfer to a blender and blend until smooth.

3 Cream the butter and sugar until pale and fluffy, then beat in the fruit purée. Beat in the eggs, then fold in both kinds of flour.

4 Grease a 1.5 litre/2½ pint/6¼ cup pudding bowl and pour in the golden syrup. Spoon in the pudding mixture. Cover the top with non-stick baking parchment (parchment paper), with a pleat folded down the centre, and then with foil pleated in the same way. Tie down with string.

5 Place the bowl in a large pan and pour in enough water to come halfway up the sides of the bowl. Cover and steam for 2 hours. During this time, you may need to top up the water.

6 When ready, remove from the pan and invert the pudding bowl on to a plate. Allow to sit for a few minutes, as the rising steam helps to release the pudding. Remove the bowl and decorate the pudding with the reserved rind.

ABOVE: Home-made fruit tarts are delicious served warm or cold with custard or cream.

# Biscuits & Cookies

*Crisp, yet sometimes chewy in the middle, cookies are universally popular among all age groups.*
*Quick to make, they will be equally quick to disappear.*

DELICIOUS AND EXTREMELY versatile, biscuits and cookies must be one of the most useful of culinary inventions. More robust and less crumbly than cake, they are the perfect solution for mid-morning and afternoon breaks. Generous country cookies are the perfect solution as a stopgap for hungry children coming home after school. They're filling enough to sustain them until tea time, yet won't spoil the main meal.

The other cookie bonus is that they are fun to make and quick to bake, and so make perfect afternoon entertainment for children in the country home. They love all the mixing and creaming that baking involves – and since they often take under ten minutes to cook, even the smallest of chefs have the patience to wait for them to come out of the oven… though waiting for them to cool before eating can test anyone's patience.

## Chocolate Brownies

*Wickedly indulgent, rich, moist chocolate cookies are an all-time favourite.*

### INGREDIENTS

| | | |
|---|---|---|
| 75g/3oz dark (bittersweet) chocolate with 70% cocoa solids | 400g/14oz/2 cups caster (superfine) sugar | 115g/4oz packet dark (bittersweet) chocolate chips |
| 115g/4oz/½ cup butter | 115g/4oz/1 cup plain (all-purpose) flour | 115g/4oz/1 cup chopped walnuts |
| 4 eggs, beaten | 25g/1oz/¼ cup cocoa powder | |
| 10ml/2 tsp vanilla essence (extract) | | |

1 Preheat the oven to 190°C/375°F/Gas 5. Grease a 18 x 28cm/7 x 11in baking pan.

2 In a heatproof bowl over a pan of gently simmering water, melt the broken-up chocolate and butter. Remove the bowl from the heat and stir in the beaten eggs, vanilla and sugar. Mix well.

3 Sift the flour with the cocoa powder and beat into the chocolate mixture. Stir in the chocolate chips and walnuts. Pour the mixture into the prepared baking pan.

4 Bake for 35 minutes until set but still moist. Leave until cold. Cut into squares.

## Oat Crisp Cookies

*These oat crisp cookies are golden and wholesome – they are ideal with a mid-morning cup of coffee or with afternoon tea.*

*This makes approximately 18 biscuits.*

### INGREDIENTS

| | |
|---|---|
| 175g/6oz/1¾ cup rolled oats | 1 egg |
| 75g/3oz/½ cup light muscovado sugar | 60ml/4 tbsp sunflower oil |
| | 30ml/2tbsp malt extract |

1 Preheat the oven to 190°C/375°F/Gas 5. Lightly grease two baking sheets. Mix the rolled oats and brown sugar in a bowl, taking care to break up any lumps in the sugar. Add the egg, sunflower oil and malt extract, mix well, then leave the mixture to soak for 15 minutes.

2 Using a teaspoon, place small heaps of the mixture well apart on the baking sheets. Press the heaps into 7.5cm/3in rounds with the back of a dampened fork.

3 Bake the biscuits for 10-15 minutes until golden. Leave them to cool for 1 minute. Lift them from the tray with a palette knife and put them on a wire rack to cool.

## Chunky Pecan Chocolate Drops

*If you want these classic cookies to have that wonderful slightly bendy, gooey texture, remove them from the baking (cookie) sheet before they are totally cool. This recipe makes 18.*

### INGREDIENTS

175g/6oz plain (semisweet) chocolate

115g/4oz/½ cup unsalted (sweet) butter, chopped

2 eggs

90g/3½ oz/½ cup caster (superfine) sugar

50g/2oz/¼ cup light brown sugar

40g/1½ oz/⅓ cup plain (all purpose) flour

25g/1oz/¼ cup cocoa powder

5ml/1 tsp baking powder

10ml/2 tsp vanilla essence (extract)

pinch salt

115g/4oz/1 cup pecans, toasted and coarsely chopped

117g/6oz/1 cup chocolate chips

115g/4oz fine quality white chocolate

115g/4oz fine quality milk chocolate

1 Preheat the oven to 160°C/325°F/Gas 3. Grease two baking (cookie) sheets. In a heatproof bowl set over hot water, melt the plain chocolate and butter. Remove from the heat, and set aside to cool.

2 Using an electric whisk, beat the eggs and sugars for about 2 minutes, until creamy. Pour in the melted chocolate mixture, beating until well blended. Beat in the flour, baking powder, cocoa, vanilla essence and salt. Stir in the nuts and chocolate.

3 Drop tablespoonfuls of mixture on to the baking sheets and bake for 8–10 minutes until crisp. Remove the baking sheets to a wire rack for 2 minutes, then transfer the cookies to a wire rack to cool.

# Sweets & Candies

*Indulge in home-made sweets, prepared with pure ingredients, then garnished with garden fruits, nuts and flowers. They are wonderful treats for the family and make great gifts, too.*

S WEETS ARE THE ultimate treats, so being able to make your own from the finest ingredients seems almost magical. They are, of course, far superior to all but the most expensive you can buy, being free from artificial preservatives and colourings, especially if you use chocolate with a minimum of 70 per cent cocoa solids. Fresh ingredients mean that these sweets don't have the long shelf life of their manufactured cousins, and many need to be kept refrigerated. If making sweets for yourself seems a little too self-indulgent, make up boxes full of them as gifts for friends, family and neighbours, or to sell at village or school fêtes. Chocolates garnished with crystallized rose petals straight from the garden, or sweet and creamy fudge and old-fashioned coconut ice, reminiscent of traditional country fairs, are always a popular draw. Make them up in large batches so you can quickly fill a stall, then package them up in cellophane, glycine paper or beautiful little boxes lined with coloured tissue. Use country raffia, twine or pretty ribbon trimmings to tie them up for a delightful gift presentation.

LEFT: Coconut ice is a mouthwatering sweet treat and is a simple combination of butter, sugar and coconut. These neat cellophane parcels tied up with a piece of green raffia make a pretty gift.

RIGHT: Chunks of flavoured, fruity or nutty fudge can be decorated to make a delicious assortment of treats. Fudge keeps well in an airtight tin.

## Chocolate Nut Clusters

*These delicious chocolate clusters make a self-indulgent tea-time treat or an elegant after-dinner accompaniment to the coffee. Use your favourite nuts in this recipe or a combination of different ones. This recipe makes 30.*

### INGREDIENTS

*550ml/18 fl oz/2½ cups double (heavy) cream*

*25g/1oz/2 tbsp unsalted (sweet) butter, chopped*

*350ml/12 fl oz/1½ cups golden (light corn) syrup*

*200g/7oz/1 cup caster (superfine) sugar*

*90g/3½ oz/scant ½ cup light brown sugar*

*pinch of salt*

*15ml/1 tbsp vanilla essence (extract)*

*425g/15oz/ 3¾ cups hazelnuts, pecans, walnuts, Brazil nuts or unsalted peanuts*

*400g/14oz plain (semisweet) chocolate, chopped*

*25g/1oz/2 tbsp white vegetable fat (shortening)*

1 Lightly oil two baking (cookie) sheets. Put the double cream, unsalted butter, golden syrup, caster sugar, brown sugar and salt in a heavy pan, over a medium heat. Stir until the butter melts and the sugars dissolve.

2 Bring the liquid to the boil and cook, stirring frequently for 1 minute until the caramel reaches 119°C/238°F (soft ball stage) on a sugar thermometer. Remove the pan from the heat and place in a bowl of cold water to stop cooking. Keep stirring to stop the mixture burning and sticking to the pan.

3 Allow the liquid to cool slightly, then stir in the vanilla essence and nuts. Remove the pan from the water. Using an oiled tablespoon, drop spoonfuls of the mixture on to the prepared sheets, about 2.5cm/1in apart. Refrigerate the trays for about 30 minutes until the mixture has hardened. Transfer the nut clusters to a wire rack.

4 Melt the chocolate and white vegetable fat in a pan over a low heat, stirring all the time until the mixture is completely smooth. Allow to cool slightly, then, using a fork, dip each cluster into the chocolate, shake off the excess and place on a wire rack over a baking sheet for at least 2 hours until completely set. Once they have set, keep them in a cool place, stored in an airtight tin.

RIGHT: Home-made chocolates and truffles taste heavenly and look exquisite. If you like, experiment with different flavourings, such as brandy, rum or coffee. Decorate them with crystallized flower petals, candied fruits, or swirls and spirals in a different-coloured chocolate. Finally, present them prettily in a beautiful box wrapped up with ribbon.

STRAWBERRIES

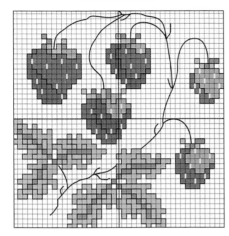

KEY

- ■ 862 dark green
- ■ 266 olive green
- ■ 243 bright green
- ■ 9046 bright red
- ■ 13 dull red
- ■ 11 deep pink
- □ 907 ochre
- ◩ 266 olive green

# *Index*

afternoon tea 52–55
appliqué blanket 27

bathroom cabinet with foil 30
beaded food cover 29
birds, foil 31
biscuits and cookies 60–61
blanket, appliqué 27
boxes, leaf printed 35
bread 56–57

candies and sweets 62–63
candle table arrangement 47
candles with pressed flowers 32
chocolate brownies 60
chocolate nut clusters 63
chocolate pecan cookies 61
colour 12, 13, 14
cookies and biscuits 60–61
crafts 24–25
cross-stitch jam pot covers 29, 64
cushions 15, 19, 34

date, fig and orange pudding 59
découpage 21
desserts 58–59
dogwood heart 43
dried bean heart 49

embroidery 28-29

fabrics 16–17, 26–27
feathers 40–41
fig, date and orange pudding 59
finishes 20–21
floors 19
flowerpot frieze 21
flowers, pressed 32–33
foil birds 31
frieze, flowerpot 21

garlands 38, 42–43, 47, 48
gifts 38–39
gingham wall 13

heart-shapes 39, 42, 43, 49
herbal tussie mussie 45
herby bread 57

jam pot covers, cross-stitch 29, 64

lampshade 41
lavender heart 43
lavender trees 49

motifs 18-19

nature notebook 33

notebook 33

oat crisp biscuits 61
one-patch quilt 27
orange, date and fig pudding 59

patchwork quilt 27
pebbles and twigs 40-41
pecan chocolate drops 61
picture frame 41
pomanders 48
posies 44–45
pressed flowers 32–33
puddings 58–59

quilt, one-patch 27

rooster cushion 19

scones 55
seasonal icons 46-47
seat cover 17
sponge-printed fruit shelf edging 35
springtime garland 47
stamps 34–35
star, willow and feather 41
sticks and stones 40–41
string-trimmed tablecloth 15
sweets and candies 62–63

tablecloth, string-trimmed 15
tea time 52–55
teabreads 56–57
textiles 16–17, 26–27
tincraft and wirework 30–31
tray with pressed flowers 33
twigs and pebbles 40–41

walls 12, 13, 20, 21, 32
wild barley ring 42
willow and feather star 41
window box edging 31
wirework and tincraft 30–31
wreaths 38, 42–43, 47, 48

yarrow topiary 49

# *Acknowledgements*

Edward Allwright, Caroline Arber, Deena Beverley, Petra Boase, Martin Brigdale, Lisa Brown, Peter Cassidy, Stephanie Donaldson, Nicki Dowey, James Duncan, Tessa Evelegh, Joanne Farrow, Lucinda Ganderton, Michelle Garrett, Andrew Gillmore, Amanda Heywood, Janine Hosegood, Karin Hossack, Tim Imrie, Paul Jackson, Alison Jenkins, Maria Kelly, Gilly Love, Mary Maguire, Leean Mackenzie, Peter McHoy, Charlotte Melling, Terence Moore, Gloria Nicol, Thomas Odulate, Lizzie Orme, Debbie Patterson, Patzi, Spike Powell, Graham Rae, Russell Sadur, Deborah Schneebeli-Morrell, Andrea Spencer, Lesley Stanfield, Isabel Stanley, Lucinda Symons, Adrian Taylor, Helen Trent, Linda Tubby, Ju Ju Vail, Liz Wagstaff, Stuart and Sally Walton, Josephine Whitfield, Elizabeth Wolf-Cohen, Mark Wood, Polly Wreford